TALKING ABOUT

YOUNG

LESBIANS

edited
by

Lorraine Trenchard

LONDON GAY TEENAGE GROUP

I would like to dedicate this to Trill, Anni, Steph and Julie.

Published by the London Gay Teenage Group
6-9 Manor Gardens, Holloway Road, N7

©1984 London Gay Teenage Group

ISBN: 0 9509455 1 X

Typeset by Bread 'n Roses, 2 St Paul's Road, London N1
Printed by Trojan Press, 10a Bradbury Street, London N16 8JN

Foreword

When writing the initial report on the research which was carried out during 1983 about the needs and experiences of young lesbians and gay men, we were aware that in bracketing the sexes together, we were ignoring the different experiences of each group. In this report young lesbians talk about themselves, and their experiences; about being young and lesbian.

Living in a society which is dominated and designed by men is difficult for any woman. Sex-role stereotyping puts pressure on young women to conform to the wife/mother image, to have a boyfriend, get married, have children. A woman's value as an individual is often measured in terms of these roles. The institutions of this society reflect and reinforce these attitudes.

Women, whether lesbian or heterosexual, are not seen as having a positive and independent sexuality. Again, women's sexuality is seen only in relation to men and the role they play in those relationships. Lesbians are therefore seen to exist in a sort of sexual vacuum. Historically, lesbians have never been recognised or given credence. Too often they are lumped under the umbrella of 'homosexuality', and once there, not given further consideration. Gay men are often given more attention and the issues which concern them are deemed to concern all homosexuals. Generalisations are made about what homosexuals are, what they do, what they want, but this is with reference to male homosexuals. These generalisations often don't consider that 'homosexual' also encompasses lesbians. This lack of visibility is another factor which separates the experiences of the sexes, and makes it more difficult for lesbians living in this society. For this reason the word lesbian will be used in this text. It is specific and, I think, positive.

There is a further factor which needs to be taken into account. Not only are young lesbians fighting for acknowledgement in a society which is male orientated, and which has denied lesbianism, but they are fighting against the power that older people have, and young people don't. It is not only a fight for a voice in an adult society, but a fight to be respected in decisions they make about themselves. Too often we met with the repeated experience of young lesbians being told that their sexuality was 'just a phase' and that they would grow out of it. The process involved in reaching the conclusion of being lesbian in a society as described above is often difficult and traumatic, and the opinion of any young person about such a personal and integral part of themselves needs to be accepted. It is an attempt to be recognised and appreciated for what they are and not just what society wants them to be.

Throughout this project I have been constantly encouraged and amazed by the strength of these young women. Despite negative attitudes, prejudice, ignorance and opposition from society, they have emerged as strong young women who are very positive about their sexuality, whatever their struggle to get to that point. This report has been possible because of these young women. They have given their time either filling out the initial questionnaires, or for subsequent in-depth interviews (or both).

On a more pragmatic level, the report owes its existence to the help, advice and support of the steering committee. Louie Hart, Micky Burbridge, Quentin Charatan, Martin Collins, Chris Heaume and Jonathan Walters. To the patience and support of my co-worker Hugh Warren who coped with my office panics. To Judy Wilkinson who coped with those panics I took home.

It also owes its existence to the Greater London Council for their continued funding so that these follow-up reports could be produced.

Thanks and acknowledgements also to Sue Lishman for designing the covers for the series and to Trilli and Diane Pacey for graphics.

Contents

Introduction

This booklet is about young lesbians. It will not tell you how to recognise a young lesbian, or how to tell if you are one. Feelings don't work like that, there aren't any 'right answers'. This is a collection of experiences, thoughts and feelings of a number of young women who have been through a variety of experiences, perhaps some will be similar to your own. It doesn't have the answers, just some of the routes young women have taken to feeling positive about being lesbians (or bi-sexual).

One of the findings of the previous report[1] was the need for positive information for young women who were questioning their sexuality. This is about young lesbians and is written, in the main, by them. It does not try to justify their existence, merely record it. In the text the quotes and accounts are not ordered in any way, not all reflect the same attitudes or views, but each experience is of equal importance. Hopefully other young lesbians will be able to identify with the experiences of these women, and realise that they're not the 'only one in the world'.

This booklet is aimed at young women questioning their sexuality, there is no apology for that, but hopefully it will help others (whether older lesbians or gay men, or heterosexual family, friends or people who work with young lesbians) to understand more about what it means to be a young lesbian. Too often what is written about young lesbians is written by self-proclaimed experts who analyse and give reasons for lesbianism. The only experts on what it is like to be young and lesbian are young lesbians.

---

1. "Something To Tell You . . .": The experiences and needs of young lesbians and gay men in London, by Lorraine Trenchard and Hugh Warren, 1984.

Who are lesbians?

Living in a society which is geared towards heterosexuals (or straights), most of what one hears about lesbians is from heterosexuals, what they think, or have heard lesbians are like. Most of the books in schools and other libraries which have any mention of lesbians are written by heterosexuals, mainly men. There isn't *one* answer to the question 'who are lesbians', because lesbians come from all groups, and backgrounds. You can't tell if a woman walking down the street is a lesbian. If you are a lesbian no-one will automatically be able to see that, you usually have to tell them. Most people don't think about homosexuality or lesbianism. They just presume that every woman is 'straight'.

These are some of the things which make it difficult for young women who are attracted to other women. What straights think lesbians are like are usually generalisations or stereotypes. When someone says "*All* lesbians are butch, or masculine" that is a stereotype and untrue. If you are just questioning your sexuality and someone says that lesbians are such and such and you *know* that you are not like that, then it is difficult to be positive about being a lesbian. You can't identify with society's stereotypes.

As lesbians don't grow horns or flashing neon signs, it is often difficult to find someone who is lesbian and will be able to tell you what it means to them. Lesbians, because of this, remain 'invisible' in a straight society. If all the lesbians in the country were to grow horns for one day you'd be very surprised not only at how many lesbians there are, but how many you actually know.

The 136 lesbians who answered our questionnaire varied as much as any group of young people. They ranged in age from 15 to 20. They were from all racial groups (in our survey mainly white), had a range of religions and beliefs from Muslim to Pantheist (of those who had a religion, most were C of E.). They came from all social classes (in our survey mainly working class — about half of the young women said that they were working class). Four of the young lesbians had been married, (one of these was still married, two separated, one divorced). Six had some sort of disability. About half of the young women had always lived in London, of those who moved to London, one third moved here because they were lesbian.

49 (37%) of the young women lived with their parents, 43 (32%) lived with lesbian or gay friends or with their lovers). Of the 136 women who answered the questionnaire 12 were still at school, 35 were at college, 44 were employed, 43 unemployed and 2 were doing YTS schemes. Even the way they defined their sexuality differed: 74 said that they were completely lesbian, 23 said that they were mostly lesbian, 29 said that they were bi-sexual, and 4 said that they were mostly heterosexual. It would be impossible to say, even from the descriptions of those who answered our questionnaire (and that is only a small proportion of the total number of young lesbians in London) what *a lesbian* is like. Below are photographs of some of the young lesbians who helped with this report.

What we have is a much clearer idea of what straights *think* lesbians are like. Most of these ideas are based on myths, ignorance and prejudice. There are lots of these about lesbians and lesbianism;

"Ever since I first heard the word lesbian I was fascinated, but I thought that I could never be like that after I was told that lesbians were funny people who dressed like men and acted butch. I was also told that it was abnormal and a sin. As I grew older I realised that none of this was true and started to get crushes on different members of my own sex. This time I was told by magazines that these were all part of growing up. I couldn't accept that, though, and began to feel worried and confused. I couldn't talk to my parents about it as they think it is some sort of illness."

(Written account)

"(My parents) don't understand anything to do with lesbians. I think that they think that lesbians are sick or ill. Or something terrible must have happened to them when they were kids to turn them off men." (Age 20)

"Her (My mother) first reaction was "You'd better go to the doctors about it!" This was followed by "How disgusting. Keep away from me". As if homosexuality was contagious. Now she thinks that just because I like girls, I must either hate men or want to be a man, (neither of which is true). She still doesn't understand as she still equates homosexuality with dirty old men screwing little boys up dark alleys." (Age 16).

"No-one talked to me for a year, I nearly got beaten up and all the girls thought I'd jump them." (Age 17).

"(My parents) Tried to arrange a visit to a psychiatrist and told me I'd get cancer?!!" (Age 20).

"(At school) I was treated as a pervert and a threat to other girls." (Age 20).

"(My parents said) 'You've been influenced'. " (Age 20).

"I think, like many heterosexuals they (parents) couldn't see beyond the sex for ages. They tended to think that being a lesbian just means sleeping with women, but they are beginning to understand there's more to it now." (Age 20).

"They (my family) blame it all on David Bowie, saying that he makes kids feel it's trendy to be queer. They all shut up when my Mum said 'ooh I think David Bowie's luvly'. " (Age 20).

an authority on homosexuality

Lesbians are women who want to be men.

Lesbianism can be cured, it's a sickness

many gays had a somewhat troubled or disturbed family life as children, or had unhealthy relationship with a parent or the other. They strongly ... these gays developed emotio... that their hom...

...nal sickness: Homosexu... is a kind of emotional illness caused by problems th... ...d with his or her parents while growing up. . it's the fau...

Lesbians are all ...d with his ... a faulty or distorted relationship between the growing child and one or both parents ...sult as a result of ...ement ...mptom of them ...al.

to all versions of the emo... ...ss theory. Many researchers have described the vari... ...f parent-

Lesbians are forever trying to seduce little girls

Lesbians are all on the ...dole and sponging off the state ...hate men

...that gays are sick.

Sometimes a mother is too domine... father is too domineering; perhaps ...e mother is col... and unloving, or the father is.

Lesbians are ... Lesbians ALL live at Greenham

Congenital defect: Homosexuals are born that way, not because of heredity; instead, something went wrong with their nervous systems while they were developing in the womb. Homosexuality is natural, but it isn't as natural as heterosexuality. Homosexuality is the result of a

Hormone imbalance. ...hormo... disorder of the endo... ...mosexuality the sex hormones with ... glands, the gland... mones, a lesbia... ...ay man hasn't ...sn't enough female hormones.

Lesbians are women who ...

Lesbians are career women

Lesbians are women who grew ...

But a great many straight peop... ...behavior they see or hear about seems den...ry, ...eculiar, unusual behavior we commonly call nurture...

Running away from it all: A homos... who can't face the challenges of bei... or at home. A lesbian is a femal... woman, wife, and mother.

...reed up." For example: the diesel dyke dressing up without sisters in a

...an at work ...s afraid to be a ...an treatment

A lesbian has a male female body.

consider it the result of faulty ...they need ...emotional development. In his view ...ill, ...osexual was a person who remained st...lly at early stage of psychological growth and ...went on to the later ones!

All lesbians are feminists ...it is on... ...l orientation dis... ...eflected chou... ...not a Lesbians ALL wear dungarees

Lesbians are mentally ill,

U... ...tly, most psychologists and psychia... ...went further Lesbians are women who don't have or want children an emotional sickness. Some found evidence in their pa-

Lesbians ALL wear three piece suits
All lesbians are middle class

many oth... turbance"—a D... ...chological illness.

Unattractiveness: If people are unattractive to persons of the other sex, they're li...

...rounds homosexuals if ...round them or have homo-

Sex Lesbians are ... ...regation: People have to live in close conta... own sex and learn to prefe...

...become like p... de...

...als if ...ies op... ...ers girls

So while it's ...
wom Lesbians are all ...apart fr... deal of homosexual behavio... homosexuality Lesbians a... Lesbians are women wh... Lesbians ALL wear tw...

Heredity: Homosexu... tary like eye color or skin

can't get a man

turn into homo... ...s seduce them.

● DIANE.

All lesbians are older (op...

LESBIANS ARE FAB!!

lesbians are white

11

Stereotypes and myths often try to explain why some women are lesbians eg "they've had a bad experience with a man", "they want to be men". Although in these examples, lesbianism is explained in terms of women's relationship to men, other myths favour a more medical view (heredity, hormone imbalance, mental illness), or a psychological view (dominant mother, faulty emotional development, no sisters). If these don't seem to fit, then they say perhaps lesbians are unattractive and "can't get a man", or have been seduced or influenced. All of these theories try to give a reason why lesbians exist. To lesbians these explanations may seem quite amusing. They reflect the need for straights to explain why some women have different sexual orientation. Men may feel threatened by the fact that not every woman's sexual preference is them; that a woman can choose to live a very happy and fulfilled life without washing her husband's socks.

These theories, however, are often very harmful. They make people see lesbianism as sick, wrong or unnatural and therefore, lesbians as women who need help, pity or "a good screw". They are also often harmful to young lesbians who feel that there must be something wrong with them if they are attracted to other women. It makes them feel bad about themselves and their sexuality. Sometimes this can be fatal. Many young women had attempted suicide because they were lesbian (one in five of the young women in our survey), and who knows how many succeeded in their attempts?

If society in general would accept that people's 'sexual preference' was not always for the opposite sex, it would make for a more healthy and accepting society. Homosexuality is not a problem, other people's reaction to it is.

"Society is geared towards heterosexuals which isn't totally a bad thing, except anyone who veers from the norm (not just sexually) is picked out. Society must be re-educated into understanding and tolerance." (Age 17).

"I am very happy being a lesbian but I just wish that society would accept us and gay men. I mean, honestly, why do they think it's a crime to love someone? They think we spend 24 hours a day in bed. Why?" (Age 18).

So, lesbians are women from every background and with many different experiences. They grow up in societies where there is little information about lesbianism, and what information there is is often negative. What one first learns about lesbianism would sometimes be enough to put anyone off. Sometimes, as this is the only information, young women believe it and feel terrible about their sexuality, like Nikki whose story you can read in chapter 5. She felt so bad about liking women that she seriously considered having a sex change operation. No one told her that it wasn't because of a hormone imbalance, (hormones only affect your sex drive, not which sex you are attracted to). In fact no one told her anything positive about being a lesbian, she had to find out for herself.

So if you're exploring your sexuality how would you know if you were a lesbian? You won't grow a second head or a tail, so how can you tell? Trust your feelings. Sometimes it helps to talk to friends, sometimes it helps to talk to lesbians (lots of young women phone lesbian line[1] to discuss just this sort of thing), it might also help to meet a few lesbians (there are a number of young lesbian groups). So long as you have the space to explore and make sense of your own emotions, don't let anyone else try and tell you how you feel or what you are. There are lots of young (and older) lesbians who have spent years of unhappiness trying to be something they're not.

The rest of this report will be about the experiences of young lesbians in different parts of their lives.

1. There is a list of lesbian lines in appendix 1.

Talking About Parents

Most young people grow up in some kind of family, whether that is single-parent, a nuclear family, or even an extended family. Members of one's family are usually very important to an individual, because of this they can also cause the most hurt or worry to a lesbian daughter/sister if they react badly. They can also be a great source of comfort and support. As one young woman said — "if your family is behind you then you can do anything and cope with anything." Seven out of every ten of the young women who answered the questionnaire had told at least one member of their family that they were lesbian.

In the questionnaire we asked "If your parents know . . . How did they react then? How do they feel now?" As you will see, lots of parents reacted badly at first but have now changed their tune. (Parents first reaction is in *italics*, and the way they feel now in normal type).

Shocked. . .
Alright, they don't mention it. Pretend it's a phase. (age 19)

My mother didn't speak to me for about 3 weeks!!. . .
I think that they accept me because they love me. But they would rather I was heterosexual (age 19)

My mum she don't mind because it's my life and if I'm happy that's what counts. . .
My mum has met my ex-girlfriend and some of my friends (age 19)

Refused to talk about it much, cried a bit, now pretends I'm not and it was just a phase. . .
Ignore my sexuality entirely, but are same as usual with me in other ways. They love me. (Age 20)

Wonderfully but slightly concerned about my happiness, believed in some myths about lesbians until I talked a lot with her about it. . .
She totally accepts it and respects my decision (age 17)

14

"Very upset — tried to finish it by court injunction. I became very distant from them . . .
Fine — let me live as I want to, try to understand me as best they can. Accept the situation and take an interest in my romances, proud to take me and my girlfriend out socially." (Age 20)

"Shock, broken hearted . . .
Now they are more understanding and are trying their hardest to accept me." (Age 18)

"(My mother said) 'Was it something that I did'. 'How can we tell the family' etc
Accept it more or less, girlfriend welcome home." (Age 20)

"My sister said 'we all know you're a bloody lesbian!' I sat down and told them it was love not lust . . .
My mother accepts it, although I think she still hopes it's a phase. The only one she blames is the one I first went out with. I keep trying to tell her that I'd be gay anyway. If it's in you, it's in you. I can tell my mum anything, from sex to anything. I feel totally at ease now, and it's so much better — now they know. Everything used to be bottled up inside me. I just wanted to tell the world that I had found love in a woman. I got bad tempered because I couldn't." (Age 20)

"IT'S LOVE, NOT LUST!"

They reacted very understandingly towards me, but did not like the idea...
They have accepted me properly now, not for what I am but because I am human like them. (Age 18)

Angry...
Accept, but ignore the fact. (Age 20)

Positively...
GREATTT!!! (Age 20)

Really understanding. My mum is brill...
Really happy, I go and visit her with my lover, and always have with lovers. (Age 17)

Very anti
Still very anti (age 20)

They didn't mind. They said it was my choice...
Fine (Age 17)

Shock and disgust...
Still shocked and disgusted — 'not normal'. They've accepted it though and are talking to me. (Age 18)

They said it was a phase
Getting used to it (age 16)

Understanding. Slightly embarrassed
They'd rather I had a boyfriend. (age 19)

Very shocked called me a lot of unpleasant things and had me put into care.
I don't know we don't discuss it (age 18)

Tried hard to be nonchalant — thought I'd grow out of it etc. Pleased, concerned but confused and uncertain.
Same only more so (age 20)

Cried
I don't know (I got thrown out of home). (Age 19)

My Dad said that I should be locked up and I was sick, my Mum cried a lot but is slowly coming to terms with it — I think...
I don't talk to my dad so I don't know — my Mum isn't too bad. (Age 16)

They went berserk and they think they have split us up...
They feel as if it is all over and done with and just a phase I was going through, but it isn't. (Age 16)

My mother got drunk — tried to beat me up and my father asked me to leave...
Fine. They want to be part of my life, they love my girlfriend and they understand. (age 20)

Very reasonably as I had been very depressed before accepting I was gay and they accept that this was the reason...
They seem to be concerned/interested in gay rights generally. (Age 20)

I cried when I told my mum (I was 14) because I was so scared what she'd say but she was fine about it — relieved in fact, cos she thought I was going to tell her I was pregnant. . .

Alright — but I never talk to my mum about being a dyke but I think that's cos I'm too shy to — she wouldn't mind if I did. (Age 17)

My mother was very supportive, although I think she thought it was a phase at first. My step-dad said that he could cope because I was a girl but he woudn't like it in a son. . .

For a long time my step-dad thought I was a member of a 'sick minority' but now he can see I am happy and settled albeit in a lifestyle he can't understand. He no longer thinks of lesbians as automatically unhappy. My mother told me of a lesbian relationship in her past. She is happy that I am happy and has some understanding of the politics involved, probably because of her past. (age 20)

I told my mum I was in love with a woman. Mum wanted me to do a test to 'make sure' — she thinks I'll be unhappy as a lesbian and blames herself. Dad told her he thought it's not so bad nowadays. . .

I think mum still blames herself, although I've explained the politics, still thinks it's not really 'natural'. She's glad to see I'm happy as a dyke. (Age 19)

My mother went crazy and behaved as if I was doing her some great injustice. I had let her down and she felt unable to cope with my sexuality alone and had to find someone to talk with. She seemed to find plenty of people! She felt I was disgusting and could only hate the woman supposedly seducing me and wouldn't allow her in the house. She blamed herself. My father has never been particularly involved and has never reacted in any way. . .

My mother has now come round to a position of complete acceptance and support. Only a few months after her initial disgust, she offered to pay for my girlfriend and I to spend a weekend in Paris for my 18th birthday present. My girlfriend and always sleep together at my house and my mother wanders in and chats to us and even sometimes brings us morning tea in bed!

My girlfriend and I sit around hugging and my mother isn't bothered. She sometimes comments on how it could be so good to love a woman and not a man as you could understand each other better. She is happy for me, for us. She commented on how she had never known me to be so happy before. (age 19)

Mum was upset, my Dad kicked me out of their home and disowned me.
The same as when I told them. (age 18)

Some young women hadn't told their parents about their sexuality. However, almost all of those who responded to the questionnaire had given the question some thought, even if their decision was NOT to tell them. Here are some comments in answer to the question "What do you think would help you to tell them (parents) if anything?"

"A wider social knowledge so that you're not made to feel wrong or afraid of being outcast." (Age 18)

"The only thing that would help me to tell my parents would be if they found out. Then I would have to tell them. It's not that I think they would throw me out, it's just the embarrassment of it all. In my mind it's not important that they know whether I go out with a male or female. Although, at times I do want to tell them how happy I am and how in love with my girlfriend. Love is far more important whatever you may be. But somehow I'd feel embarrassed with them knowing. I think my mother knows but is trying to keep quiet." (Age 19)

"Nothing". (Age 20)

"Better publicity, more television programmes." (Age 20)

"Nothing, utterly closed minds. It would cause an irreparable rift — and I still need my grant cheque. Besides, why cause them unncessary distress. They simply would not be able to understand." (Age 20)

"I would find it helpful to know that they will still treat me the way they do now — and not as a freak. Sadly, I cannot be sure how they will react." (Age 20)

"A leaflet/any literature on lesbianism/gays which could be given to them to educate them." (Age 17)

"It would help if only my mother's attitude towards gay people wasn't one of 'Oh, they're sick'. If only she could see that they're totally normal (whatever *that* is!) people. But I just don't think she ever will, so I daren't tell her — it would hurt her so much." (Age 19)

18

So, if you are a lesbian, or think you might be, at some stage you will have to think about talking to members of your family about it. The experiences of the young lesbians in this report might be helpful to you if you do decide to tell them. You might decide, like some of the young lesbians, not to tell them. Sometimes there are very good reasons for not telling them, for instance until you leave home and are independent. Some young lesbians told their mothers (or parents) before they told anyone else. It depends very much on individual circumstances.

What the young lesbians did find quite often was that their parents hadn't thought about lesbianism before, and didn't know much about it. They found that they had a lot of educating to do, that it wasn't just a phase etc. Most parents, as was said earlier, do accept lesbianism after a while. Some parents are supportive and positive from the beginning. Whatever their feelings though, they usually expect you to bring the subject up.

You might decide to tell a friend, to "come out" at school. Young lesbians will be talking about school in the next chapter.

Talking About School

Everyone has to go to school, at least until they're 16. So you end up spending a long time in a place where you're meant to learn things, and during that process 'grow-up'. It's not just from the text books and lessons that you learn and grow, but through the people (teachers and pupils) that you get to know. Through their school years most people are exploring relationships and their sexuality. This is usually more acceptable in boys who are expected to start experimenting with sex and their bodies.

This attitude about what is accepted of boys and what is expected of girls is reflected in both the lessons and books, and by what people in schools say and how they act/react. If you're straight then it is often much easier to fit in with a system that is geared towards heterosexuals, it might not be ideal, but it's designed for you. If you are lesbian, or think that you might be, then school is sometimes a more difficult place to be. The lessons hardly ever include anything about homosexuals. Lesbianism is mentioned even more rarely. So finding out about lesbians, or talking about it in a helpful way is often difficult. The books is school libraries aren't usually helpful — if there are any there that mention lesbianism at all.

So, in schools you often can't learn about an alternative sexuality through the 'formal' channels. We learn a lot about life from the people in schools. Sometimes talking to friends about sex and sexuality can be supportive and informative. However, many young people at school tend to treat homosexuality as a joke. Calling someone a lezzie is a common insult. Like society generally, these attitudes are based on ignorance. These are the stereotypes and myths that were mentioned earlier. Of the young women who answered the questionnaire, 60% (77 out of the 130 lesbians who answered that question) said that they had friends at school who knew they were lesbian.

There might be teachers at your school who you can talk to about your sexuality, 36 (of the 130 lesbians who answered the question) said that at least one teacher at school knew that they were lesbian. Teachers might be able to find information for you, or put you in touch with someone you can talk to. Sometimes school can be a place where you can talk about lesbianism, or even meet other lesbians, 68 of the young women knew other lesbians at school, some were pupils, some were teachers. Sometimes school can be a very confusing and frightening place to be. A place where nobody else seems to feel the same as you, where emotions aren't always returned, where 'best-friends' drop you for boyfriends. It can be lonely, but remember that, statistically, one in every ten people is homosexual — so if you're in a class of thirty, the chances are that there will be at least three of you. You might find that by talking about lesbianism, you might help others to question their prejudices. You might even be helping someone who is questioning their sexuality.

Experiences at school varied for all the young lesbians we spoke to. Some didn't realise that they were lesbians until they had left school, some had relationships with school friends, some had supportive friends and teachers, some didn't tell anyone that they were lesbian, some got harassed because they did tell people. These are some of the young lesbians' experiences, and some suggestions about how things could be made easier for young lesbians and gay men at school:

"I didn't realise, or admit to myself that I was gay at school. I knew I didn't like boys, but didn't find it worrying. I became attached to one girl and we were 'best friends' for 5 years until I told her I was in love with her, or thought I was. I didn't know what I was feeling. In my final year I was a bit of a wreck, cried a lot when we argued, even missed classes because I was crying. It affected my work and teachers used to ask what was the matter. It was terrible". (Age 19)

"Homosexuality was mentioned once — in parentcraft." (Age 18)

"If people were taught more about the subject it might help them to understand, and possibly help their friends cope if they need to talk about being gay. Also, it is still classed as a 'hush hush' subject, and therefore people build up barriers and feel they are 'different' or 'wrong'. Therefore a wider understanding would help." (Age 18)

"My school was a church school. My lover was the head girl. We were very open, and they expelled me! . . .
More should be taught about the value of feelings and the scope of relationships available to people, and less should be taught about the mechanics of heterosexual sex (ie the emphasis on the idea that sex IS heterosexual intercourse.) Teachers and pastoral staff should be made to realise that the attitudes of anti-gay pupils/teachers are responsible for the 'problems' concerning being gay/lesbian and that being gay/lesbian is not a problem". (Age 20)

"At school I was mixed up. I was unable to cope with the fact that I felt/saw things differently from everyone else." (Age 20)

"For teachers, when talking about it, not just to treat being gay as just a sex thing. Not to describe gays as poofs, queers etc, as something to laugh at, degrading and something to be ashamed of. When teaching young kids sex education bring the homosexual aspect in gradually and normally, as if you're not a freak to be gay. It's hard to think you're normal, especially when everything in the media, television, adverts etc portray the happy man and woman image. Treat everyone as an individual, with different feelings, try when teaching not to generalise. It's the media and the way you're taught to think that makes you feel abnormal." (Age 19)

"(I had problems at school as a lesbian because) I wasn't interested in the social life. I was considered boring because I didn't want to go to parties. I wasn't able to talk about girlfriends." (Age 17)

"Things that immediately spring to mind — most schools have some form of sex education, all based around reproduction, and one form of heterosexual sex. If masturbation is mentioned it is as an abnormality, something you grow out of, or even as an outright 'sin'. Homosexuality is never mentioned, as if it did not exist, but you could easily conclude from the attitude to masturbation that if homosexuals do exist then they are even worse. Obviously I think that attitude is ridiculous and disgusting and must be changed.

Further, any rumour of a teacher being gay is a scandal and proof results in sacking. This attitude towards homosexuality in teachers obviously indicates that there is something very bad about it and something definitely to be hidden and to be ashamed of. If teachers could be openly gay and under no threat, not only could they give a positive image of homosexuality, but important support and information. Freedom to discuss sexuality in lesson time is very important and teachers should initiate this. Prejudiced views against homosexuals should be viewed as are racist remarks in that discrimination is factually unfounded and that it is the people making prejudiced generalisations who are ignorant or evil, not those on the butt end.

Obviously schools should stock books about homosexuals, or with gay characters positively portrayed, as well as factual information about gay groups etc. But not just written info. Books are a great turn-off to some people. There should be videos shown to classes and fact sheets available without asking, and not just from the library." (Age 19)

"Ban heterosexuals!" (Age 19)

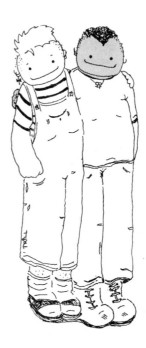

"Wider sex education — treatment of gay sexuality as an alternative, NOT a perversion. Less emphasis on reproductive sex. At my school homosexuality was NEVER discussed in human biology lessons and therefore, not surprisingly, all sorts of myths about it arose eg all lesbians like little girls. Also, better education might help to combat the common retort 'it's not natural' — I mean 'natural' means existing in nature, therefore.... Also *Rubyfruit Jungle* as an 'O' level set text! Seriously, a very straight friend of mine read it and was in hysterics throughout and subsequently proved much more tolerant." (Age 19)

"I think that other forms of sexuality as well as heterosexuality should be taught and discussed. At my school homosexuality was never mentioned unless it was in a joke. I think that it non-gays were made more aware of gays they'd come to accept us more and they might even realise that we don't go round screwing everything in a ten mile radius and that love does actually come into it too." (Age 16)

"Compulsory education on the existence of us. Most times I say 'I'm a lesbian' whoever it is. I feel like the 'first ever born in captivity' — some sort of zoological curiosity. Most people are shocked that someone they know or meet could be 'like that'. School referred me to a psychologist (?) or psychiatrist on the pretext of being 'worried about my work'. They mentioned EEG, then ECT, then I ran away from home." (Age 17)

"Attitudes amongst staff and parents needed to be changed drastically. I was treated as a pervert and a threat to the other girls. I was thrown out." (Age 20)

"No-one knew, not even me." (Age 20)

"I had no-one to talk to about being gay." (Age 19)

"Someone translated Chaucer into modern English using the word 'gay'. The English teacher made a snide comment about gay being a polluted word — I argued back. Over the next year the English teacher baited me on lesbianism every lesson and everyone thought that I was gay. One woman approached me recently, having found my stand helpful at school. (My problems at school also included) teasing, harassment, threats of violence, having my bicycle tampered with, having food thrown at me etc. It would be more pleasant/ safer for a lesbian to be at a girls-only school! I found the boys at my school very immature/threatening. They thrust centrefold porn under my nose saying offensive things like 'Cor! Don't you fancy her!'. It helped when the headmaster moved me to a different part of the school. Lesbian teachers, whether they are 'out' or 'closeted', are helpful as role-models, implicit support etc. Books in the library such as *Patience and Sarah* and *Sappho was a Right-On Woman*, NOT *Well of Loneliness*." (Age 20)

"At school there was a sense of having to deceive, ostracism etc. It would help if anti-gay teachers were chucked out. If anti-gay literature was chucked out. If we were given a positive image." (Age 18)

"No-one talked to me for a year, I nearly got beaten up, and all the girls thought I'd jump them. (It would help to have) paid protection — well, seriously I don't know — I suppose try and make it seem as normal as possible but how can you do that when the minute they think a teacher's queer she gets chucked out so s/he can't molest the children? You've got to tackle the whole fucking education system and hierarchy of school governors, heads etc, before most of them'll ever even let a feminist magazine like *Spare Rib* in the library. I don't know what to do." (Age 17)

"My so-called friends didn't believe me, then acted as if I had a 'nasty illness'. People took the micky out of me and tried to upset me. Maybe, if the topic was talked about a bit more, people would not feel so threatened by it. If it was treated as a 'normal' thing, instead of 'strange and dirty', then young gay people would not have to go through quite so much teasing and hurt, as they often do now. There should be more information available to younger people at school about homosexuality." (Age 16)

"I had problems in sixth form trying to bring my girlfriend into school activities (social) as she did not attend my school. There ought to be less sex-role stereotyping. I attended a girls' grammar school where we were not only educated, but trained to be young ladies. 'Tomboyish' behaviour was only excused if shown in sport. I needed to be shown that girls do not have to fit into one or other box. As an unathletic lesbian I had some difficulty finding my slot — no longer interested in boys, I did not fit into the genteel young lady set, and not interested in the sports lot. I drifted away from friends at school." (Age 20)

All the young women have been at a school of some sort for some of their lives, for some it was a good experience, others had a lousy time. Whatever their experiences at school, most of the young lesbians had some criticism of the way that homosexuality/lesbianism was treated (if at all), they also had a lot of constructive ideas about how things could be changed to make life easier for young lesbians in schools. These changes will probably be made very slowly, because that is how education authorities work. They might change a bit more quickly if young people (lesbians, gays and straights) start asking why. 'Why aren't we taught about homosexuality? Why aren't there any books in the library about lesbians? Feminists?' Head teachers, teachers and school governors often say that homosexuality isn't dealt with in 'their' schools because there aren't any lesbians/gay men in 'their' schools. Part of changing the system to include information about homosexuals is to convince them (the people with the power) that everyone should learn about homosexuality, that that is the way to a more caring and understanding society. They wouldn't think only teaching young people of colour about race, would they? The people you are at school with now are going to be the next generation of parents and policy makers, it is as important for them to understand about lesbians and gay men as it is for you — *their* children might be lesbian or gay, they might work with lesbians or gay men, they might run the country!

Just as with your family, you may think about telling people at your school (pupils or teachers) that you are lesbian. Again, it will depend very much on your own particular circumstances. You might decide to tell no one, or just close friends, or come out completely. If you decide not to tell any member of your family, a friend might be easier, 73 of the 121 young women who answered the questionnaire told a friend first. If you feel that you can't talk to either your family or your friends, phone one of the lesbian or gay helplines and talk to a lesbian there, it usually helps just to have a chat with a lesbian about being a lesbian. One young lesbian wrote

"I phoned lesbian line when I was 13. They gave me the confidence to come out. They were brilliant"

Talking About Themselves

JACKIE 18, & DI 20.

Di:
Even when I was 8 I used to stay over with this girl. And we used to hug and everything. That went on until I was 10, then she went to another school and she didn't want to talk about it. They've all got their boyfriends and their jobs. Then I met this girl when I was 13, and that went on until I was 16. I had boyfriends and stuff all the time because I thought I had to. That's what all the magazines and stuff said. I used to say, "I'm not going to kiss you" to them. We used to take the piss out of them. Up until I was 10 there were separate playgrounds for boys and girls. Like it was perfectly alright for you to have girlfriends. Then when you reach 12, it's all designed for you to get yourself a boyfriend.

Jackie:
I always felt really alienated at school. I just locked myself in my bedroom like a hermit for about 6 years, and I just wouldn't come out. I never went anywhere. I used to just go out for school. I didn't like school very much, but it was a necessity. It was easier after I was 11, 'cos it was an all girls school. I just felt like I didn't belong. Not ever. You really kind of withdraw into yourself 'cos you can't ever communicate. They all sit and talk about their boyfriends and I just didn't want to know. But I don't think I knew why I didn't want to know at the time. I just thought that I was a bit different. I wasn't the one they picked on and called "lezzie, lezzie". They just said, "Oh, that's Jackie and she's a bit odd." I just accepted I was a bit eccentric.

Di:
I did the opposite. Everyone used to bring 'Jackie' and those sorts of magazines. They used to scratch "John for Janet" on the desks, and I used to scratch things on the desk for them. Sort of join in. And I scratched "Val for Di" on my arm. This woman came around to look for fleas and she looked at my nails, and she saw "Val for Di" in scabs on my arm. She wrote to my parents. My Dad was brill about it. I thought he'd think this a bit odd, you know, "Val for Di". But he just said "It could have got infected!". Yeh, I used to kind of join in and read all their magazines. They were all soppy,

and I used to say, "Why is the girl like this? and the boy like that?" It was really obvious, I mean me and Val used to walk around the playground holding hands and kissing and that. They boys had this rhyme for us and I honestly didn't know what the words meant. It went:

"Two raving lesbo's, go buy a dildo"

And we used to say, "Oh no, we're not!", and not know what it meant. We got split up by the teacher, separate dinner hours and all. And we went into the headmaster and said, "why are you doing this?". We didn't understand, just thought that they didn't want us to be together. They didn't explain it, they weren't being honest with us. I really plagued the headmaster. We used to go in every day and cry and say, "Why? Why?". I mean we used to deny that we were lesbian — we didn't know what it meant and didn't think to go look it up, and we wouldn't know where anyway.

I was really ignorant about what I was feeling. It upset me the way I was picked on. I felt helpless, I didn't have any words to fight back with. We moved to another school at 14. I did look in the library at the other school 'cos I knew what it meant then, but there was never any mention of it in lessons. I used to get on really well with the boys 'cos they didn't mean anything to me.

Jackie:
I don't think I've not been a lesbian. I came out originally as a lesbian, then went back in the closet. Then I became limitedly feminist. I then realised that I had been screwing my head up all this time by trying to convince myself that I was straight.

Di:
Since I was about 16 I used to call myself a feminist but I used to say — but I'm not extreme, I don't hate people. And things like that. I don't hate men, they just don't do very much for me. I knew that I was really angry about a lot of things, but I didn't really have a label for it then, I knew I was a lesbian before that.

Jackie:

At school they mentioned it in the 6th form, in sociology. It was mentioned under deviancy. You know, lumped between murders and the insane. They always underplayed things. There was just innuendo about anything sexual.

Di:

The lads used to send us these dirty books, and it was mentioned there. But that was just the lads. At our other school I can't remember it being mentioned, not even in a joking way.

Jackie:

Amongst the girls in the 6th form it was a real topic of conversation, 'cos my friend was really out. But I wasn't identifying as lesbian then. But I was in love with my best friend who was straight.

Di:

But did you think about things like 'straight'? Like that's straight and this is gay? I didn't even think of it.

Jackie:

Yeh, I did cos there had been a lot of politicising before hand. I was involved with "Shocking Pink", that young women's magazine. I began to realise that there was a political affiliation, in some places, with lesbianism. It had never occurred to me before, I had thought it was just purely sexual, and then I finally realised that it had a lot to do with politics, and your attitude towards society and stuff like that. And how it can be a political decision not to sleep with men. I think my whole school experience was really easy. I suppose we didn't need anything in the library — I didn't look. We discussed it a lot. It was great. A lot of the women actually saw it as a viable choice. Some took it, others didn't and now they're happily engaged or whatever. But the point is — they had the choice. You can spend so many years being so miserable 'cos no one gave you the choice. They force you into doing things.

Di:

I was unsure about what I was myself, and it was unlikely that any of my friends were lesbian. I was really scared to tell them. There was a real fear of losing the circle of friends that I had, so I didn't tell them. I wasn't political. I didn't meet any women who felt the same way as me. It would have helped if there had been a book or something. But until I was 18 there was nothing. It was difficult to get anywhere, the nearest town was about 25 miles away so Mum had to take me to the station and things.

Jackie:

My parents don't know. My Mum would be happier to know, but she's not saying anything. She's waiting for me to tell her. I feel so protective of my mother, I'm just scared of hurting her in any way, shape or form. She's the most important person in my life. She gets hurt all the time.

BARBARA, 20.

I 'came out' at 14 years old and am now 20. The first girl I met (at 14) was only 13 years old and lived in the same children's home. Even at that stage I knew I preferred women. This relationship, which was very intimate, lasted thirteen months — before the 'authorities' separated us and would no longer allow me to see her. This really hurt and I would not see anyone — which lasted two years. After this time I met Tania who was at the same remand centre as me. Again, the relationship lasted two years before meeting another girl at the same hostel where I lived. (It lasted six months).

After all this I moved to Oxford and after a series of relationships, finally moved to London. Since moving to London I've been out with, and loved, a number of women, but only one person I've met means something.

CATH, 20.

I've always been attracted to women, but for years I managed to persuade myself I wouldn't be once I met 'Mr Right'! Now I've stopped hoping I'm going to change so I can really enjoy my life. My strongest memories of school are of feeling an outsider. I was at a girls' grammar school so boys were almost the only topic of conversation. I kept falling for all the women, but tried to convince myself I was only looking for a mother figure. Over several years I was madly in love with one particular (straight) woman. She introduced me to feminism and that was the start of it all. It was wonderful to be with other women and I slowly realised it was lesbian women I felt most at home with.

When I went to college I inevitably got involved with men, but couldn't understand why I was bored and always thinking of the women at home. Last summer I left the man I had been living with — I was lucky with him because I could come out to all his friends. I get very angry whenever I look back on it because of how I had to put myself down all the time to keep him happy and boost his ego — after all, he was the head of the household. In the autumn we started a Gay Soc. at college, but I didn't want to call myself gay — I don't like being dismissed with a label. Now I'm confident about my sexuality and proud that I've now felt able to accept it. It is a great relief to be able to turn my back on oppressive heterosexual ways of life. I don't need to compromise my feminism because I have to hold on to my man at all costs.

I've told my closest friends and it didn't bother them at all — I had been worried they would think I was after them. I don't think I can tell my parents — not because I am ashamed or frightened, but because I know how upset they would get. It would make a big difference though, if I felt they would accept me no matter what.

ELLEN, 15.

At the age of 8 I was playing mummy and daddy with a friend and we got into bed together. We became so involved in our enjoyment of touching each other that we forgot we were playing a game. Another friend was with us and when we asked her to get into bed with us, she said what we were doing was bad and she went home crying. From then on, touching another girl in any sort of affectionate way seemed bad and wrong. But that didn't stop me from doing so.

I had some really good experiences. One girl became my best friend. We spent the afternoon in my bedroom and had a great time. We kissed and cuddled and rubbed our bodies together and touched and masturbated and thoroughly enjoyed ourselves. My feelings were over-powering. I loved her and she loved me. We felt what we were doing was pretty natural and felt so good, but we were scared as hell if anyone might find us. I never saw her again after that week.

When I was 14, I was invited to stay with another friend. We stayed up late every night watching her video of 'Fame'. She was in love with Lee-Roy. God, it was awful. One night I had a backache and she opted to massage it for me. She practically tickled me to death, but she turned me on too. When we eventually went to bed together, I had to play as if I was Lee-Roy and she was my girlfriend. It was funny and a good laugh, but disgusting.

You'd have thought I would have learnt not to get myself into such a situation. But no, I got myself stuck again, this time for a few months. Somewhere between 14 and 15 years. I started to play a stupid game called Camilla and Dean with a friend who lived a couple of doors away from me. I always played the male even though I hated it so much. She was 10 at that time, had no boyfriends and was craving for some sexual experience. So was I, but with a real GIRLFRIEND. She used me. I used her. When I told her I thought I was a lesbian, I think she panicked because we never played that game again. God, I was relieved.

OK so that's all my sexual experiences. Some people would put that down as child and teenage natural feelings. Fine! But then they say "you'll grow out of it." My parents said that when they found out. God, I was mad. I don't want to grow out of it.

At around the age of 12, my aunt started talking about feminism with me. We'd stay up really late just talking and debating about such things as society's view on feminists and stereotypes and girls and boys and lesbians and contraceptives etc. My aunt is a feminist, not a lesbian. She's a great friend. She's not quite how you'd imagine an aunt to be — like stern and always knowing what's best for you. She's understanding and sympathetic, out-going, bouncy and a constant pillar of strength and advice. After all those good points, I can only think of one bad point: she's grumpy in the morning unless you make her a cup of tea. Anyway, I've learnt a lot from her. When I told her I thought I was gay, she said, "If that's what makes you happy, great!" Then we talked about the problems I might face and how good it will be. Although I had more or less known at 12, I did not tell her till I was 14.

I had to decide whether to come out of the closet or not. I wrote a list of my closest friends and started thinking about how I would tell them. I was drawn between two ideas, I thought, "Well, I want them to know because it would be nice to be myself for a change instead of having to go out with boys just to prove I'm one of the girls. Also they might think 'my friend is gay so it can't be as bad as people make out, because she's alright'." But, if what I thought were my friends didn't turn out to be that friendly, and spread it to people or places where it would be held against me, then I wasn't coming out. God, what a decision. But I feel really good about something that's really good, I've got to tell it to people sooner or later or I go crazy with frustration. Well, *that* decided for me. As I was going to tell others now, I felt I had to be positive about it to others or they might dismiss it or be nasty about it.

The first friend I told got really scared as I had built it up so much over a few weeks. One of our conversations went something like this:
Me: There's something about me you don't know and I don't think you're going to like it.
Her: Tell me.
Me: You'll probably be really disgusted.
Her: No, I won't. What is it?
Me: Oh God! I don't know how to put it.
Her: Just blurt it out. I'll try not to be shocked or anything.
Me: I can't. But put it this way. If my parents find out, I'm finished.
Her: Is it that bad?
Me: It depends on how you take it.

Her: God! You're not pregnant, are you?
Me: no.
Her: Are you on drugs?
Me: No.

These sort of dramatic scenes went on for about three weeks on and off. Eventually she asked, "Have you murdered somebody?" When the answer was "No" yet again, my friend was in the depths of despair. She'd totally run out of ideas. I felt so sorry for her. I was really putting her through it. The next day I went round to her house and she said "Are you a lesbian?" I said "Yep!!"
Her: IS THAT ALL?!!
Me: Yep!!
She burst out laughing.

I've told about 8 of my friends. Like I said, only my closest friends, but I didn't tell the others like I told the first. With the rest I just said it when I thought it was the right place at the right time. They all didn't seem to care one way or the other. In fact they started asking me all sorts of weird and wonderful questions, most of which I couldn't answer anyway, but I was really glad I came out to them. One of my friends still argues with me occasionally. She's convinced it's just a phase I'm going through, but she's not really bothered. Coming out felt great. I wanted to run down the street shouting it out, but I couldn't bring myself to do that.

I've had boyfriends in the past, not only because I wanted to keep in with my peers, but also to find out what my feelings towards boys were. At the moment the only feelings I've got for boys is sympathy. When I kissed them, I felt like being sick.They put on a whole performance as if it was something out of Romeo and Juliet. It's like kissing mouldy cheese. Going out with them isn't much fun either. They go around like they own you and you're supposed to be grateful. I've never lasted more than 2 weeks with a boy, thank God! Boys get attracted to me because I seem independent, but after they've had a taste of my so-called independence, they get scared or put off. I usually chuck them tho' before they do me, I made an advance to a boy once (asked him out) but I never flirted with them. Waste of time and bother. One boy I went out with, I told him I was a lesbian (in a hope to get rid of him). He didn't bloody care and I couldn't shake the silly sod off. The next night he came round to my house at 12.30am without any warning whatsoever, to ask me out. I just flipped and that was that. I have not seen him since.

One hot, sunny, beautiful day, my mum found this letter in my room. Of course she showed it to my dad. My dad didn't have an inkling, but mum said she had had a faint idea because of some things I had said and done. I really thought that they'd be mad, but they didn't say a thing. I think they just didn't want to acknowledge it. I was the one who brought it up. They were sitting in the garden and looked all sort of worried about something. They were whispering too. I knew my letter had been found. I wondered how I was going to approach them. I thought of going up to them, kneeling at their feet, putting my head on Mum's knee and saying "Don't worry, it's not yours or anybody's fault. I'm happy and you've always said that's all that matters." But I'm not like that. Soggyfied or what? Anyhow, if I did something like that my parents would see it as being really cheeky and stupid. So I walked up to them and said "Hey, listen! I know you know, but before you get worked up and all that, I think we ought to have a good honest talk." Something like that. We talked for about 2 hours. These are the sorts of questions they fired at me:

Who's to blame? Have you ever had a bad experience with a man and not told us? Have we brought you up wrong? Have we failed somewhere along the line? Why? How? How do you know for sure? What was wrong with boys? Is that why you always wear trousers; don't shave your legs; don't wear make-up; are a tom-boy? Have you ever had any real relationships with girls? If not, why are you telling us you're a lesbian? Have you told the rest of the family? And friends? Anyone else? So you've told some friends. What if it gets to their parents? Have you thought about the effects that would have on your friendships? Have you considered our reputation? What if it gets out all round the little country town we live in? You know what friends are like and some could turn nasty. What about your future? If it gets out at where you work or whatever, then you know you can be sacked because of it? Why don't you just give it up? You'll find society isn't too good towards lesbians. Why don't you just be normal and live your life how you're expected to? It'll be much easier and much happier. We know you'd say no to a psychiatrist, but what about a youth Counsellor?

God! Millions of questions and millions of answers.

The: "Come back at 21 and tell us you're still a lesbian, but at 15 we find it a bit hard to believe." I'd kept my cool up until then. You can stand only so much!

I guess I started questioning life and the way I was living mine, when I started having those deep discussions with my aunt. Before then I'd never linked up my feelings for girls with lesbianism. I even joined in with the laughs and jokes about them at school. Now, I am a feminist I guess. It feels weird labelling myself like that, but then, I label myself in career terms too.

I'm 15 at the moment, still at school and I guess like most kids my age, thinking a lot about the future.

I don't think I've ever liked the idea of marriage or children. I adore kids and I get on really well with them, but I don't think I could abide some of my own. I'm the sort of person who likes to do things (out of the home) so the thought of being tied down with children does not appeal to me. I wouldn't mind working with them though. I already do a bit and I really enjoy it. I once wrote out a list of the good points and the bad points of having children. Even though the bad points over-ruled the good ones, I still think it's wonderful to have children. I still think I'd much rather have a career than children. Is that selfish? I don't know.. Maybe I'm too young to take it so seriously anyway. I'll consider it again when I'm 25.

Feminism and lesbianism is already a large part of my lifestyle and it will probably remain that way for the rest of my life. I love it. It makes me feel good. I guess it's Living-Life-to-the-Full.

FIONA, 17

Asked to write about the subject of coming out I find myself asking the questions: 'When did I come out? Have I come out?' I have done to a certain extent, and I know that every day I shall continue.

Looking back, at the age of 13 years old at school, I had a very close friend who visited me at my sickbed. I was generally being comforted by her presence. Somehow she ended up in bed with me. Being a curious adolescent, she decided to see whether or not I liked my nipples being touched, and soon explored other parts of the body. At the time I was too shocked by her advances to enjoy the sensation I now feel with women. This incident lessened our friendship because at the time I was confused. So at 13 I was not defined as a lesbian.

At 15, a very controversial issue which was always being raised between my clique of friends was gayness. Of course we had our suspicions. Unlike the experience of most people, being gay was quite OK with my friends, and none of them denied the fact that they could be as many of us had not had experiences with either sex so considered it too early to judge and did not suppress our attractions for people of the other sex.

Whilst having tremendous support from school, I also had a friend who I was very close to and one day she came out and told me she was a lesbian. I was not shocked at all, I already knew many gay men and women due to working in the theatre. Shortly after her 'Coming-Out' she was thrown out of her home by her non-accepting parents. So as my mother was away, I put her up for a few nights until everything blew over. On our first night together we went to 'Stallions' where I met a girl who I became very good platonic friends with. I explained to her that I was not ready to confirm my sexuality being a very unsure 16 year old. I knew this girl for 3 weeks when I moved in with her. Even though she had a girlfriend, my mother had to think we were having an affair, but she did nothing to discourage it. I was by then sure that I was gay, yet had only slightly come out to her by telling her I go to gay clubs, have gay (male) friends etc. But when asked frequently if I was a lesbian I told her I was bi-sexual. She once had doubts about letting me go to a party 40 miles from home, but as soon as I told her it was gay she let me go. My mother has great faight in me which I would

a party 40 miles from home, but as soon as I told her it was gay she let me go. My mother has great faith in me which I would not intentionally betray.

Now I have just finished my first sexual relationship with a woman. I have not told my mother what she expects to hear, yet she said to me, 'If you're gay I'll understand, a lot of people your age go through this phase.' I have come out to my friends and as expected I have taken some stick, but eventually they realise I am still the same person. I am very lucky not to have gone through the hardship I have seen some people go through.

One day I shall come out completely, but first of all I start with you, mum.

GAIL, 18

I never realised I was a lesbian until I was almost 17. I was madly in love with my best friend at school. She didn't speak to me, decided she'd had enough of me. I sat with a gun pointed at my head. I mean, I was really far gone. I've done my wrists a couple of times. But I don't like pain and I don't like mess. Twice it was a very serious attempt, though. You know, like when you can't see a way out of what you're in and you want to end the way you're living — not your life. There's one thing about that — it's made me really anti-suicide. I don't want any bastard saying "Oh, she can't cope". I don't get depressed these days anyway.

I've had a lot of contact with the police, mainly at Greenham. A lot of it is just abuse, "you fucking lesbians, what you need is . . ." Another time I was standing at a bus stop in Brixton and this guy, I thought he was drunk, came lurching over. Turned out he was from CID and wanted to know if I was soliciting. There I was — standing in my DM's splattered with mud, and wearing dyke badges. I said I was gay and he proceeded to give me a lecture about getting mixed-up with "that sort".

HANNAH, 19.

At school I had a relationship in the upper sixth, but I didn't consider myself a lesbian. I always considered myself bi-sexual — thought it was the 'natural state' that I was getting back to. We talked about it a lot. For example we talked about the lesbian and gay centre in Islington and the other girls would say, 'What about the Irish in Islington?' It was quite difficult because it was an all girls school and we were all fairly close, so some of them felt uneasy.

I suppose it would have helped if there were books about lesbians in the library, but you've already got to be at a stage where you identify as lesbian to pick up a book. I suppose you've really got to have lesbian teachers who are open — to discuss it in lessons. And not making the assumption that everyone is heterosexual. With teachers, you identify with them as people and their sexuality is part of them. I suppose you need to have lesbian heads, lesbian governors, and lesbian ministers of education. We never discussed lesbians, like in history. We never discussed what women have done. Maybe a bit in literature, but that was mainly about men.

I define myself as a lesbian. I suppose because it's partly a political decision — it's based on reading and thinking rather than the experience of actually having heterosexual relationships. So I guess I ought to be more empirical. I'm a lesbian so I want relationships with women, but I feel I haven't had the full experience. But, yes, I define myself as lesbian.

I'm going to college in September. At present I live at home with my parents and my brother. I do identify as Jewish, not religiously, but culturally. I guess the only way it has affected my sexuality is that it's made it a bit more difficult to come out — perhaps because of the close family networks, so you're more aware of the repercussions on all the family. It's more a question of when are you getting married, and if you're going to marry 'out'. My immediate family all know that I am a lesbian, except perhaps my eldest sister who is a Freudian psychiatrist. I haven't actually told them, but I know that they know, and they know that I know they know. We sort of discuss it all the time, it's always very intellectual. We intellectualise about things which are personal. My sister is a lesbian and my mum thinks that's fine. My father finds it a bit more difficult because he's more traditional. My mum is great. If I have a friend to stay she says, 'Will you be using the double bed?' That's how she shows she knows. My father doesn't talk about that sort of thing except on an intellectual level. There wouldn't be any question of rejection if I told them, they'd just find it uneasy.

I went to a mainstream youth club when I was younger, but I found it dreadfully anti-semitic, I got beaten up. I started going to the young lesbian group mainly to see a friend of mine who went. I find it quite good fun. I mean, most of the lesbians I know are so much older, and it's quite interesting to see women my own age who are lesbians. And also, because I've seen it through being a feminist and getting there that way. It's interesting to look at lesbianism from a different perspective — most of the women there aren't feminist, or wouldn't consider themselves feminist.

Men? Personally I find them a bit boring. Not very stimulating. I think that there should be separatists, but I don't see myself as being one. I don't think that lesbianism and feminism are mutually synonymous, but I think that if you're a lesbian, then you've challenged society's norms so therefore, in a way you're a feminist because you've decided to go against them. The myth about lesbians being seduced? I don't know, I don't think it's true. If you have a relationship with someone who's 17 then you're less likely to identify it as lesbian than if you have a relationship with an older woman, because SHE'LL identify it as lesbian.

I think that part of the problem with class is that most feminists are seen as being middle class. I think most of those women who get into role playing are probably working class. They're saying you don't have to be feminist to be lesbian. They're saying fuck you to all those middle class lesbians. And also because middle class lesbians seem to have monopolised the whole idea of being a lesbian through being a feminist. It's important for other women to find a way of expressing their sexuality, as opposed to trying to be like the image of middle class lesbians.

I think that if there wasn't any political decision I'd say that I was bi-sexual.

NIKKI,20.

I was born into a Catholic family, yeh! I suppose my parents were pretty repressively Catholic. My Mum was into quite strict ways of dressing — skirts and things. I went, always to Catholic schools. I went to mass every day. Women didn't seem to amount to very much. I was a real tomboy, I used to play 'the Three Musketeers', and things. I used to really hate the girls. They seemed really soppy and used to kind of accept everything that was coming to them. They did crochet etc.

At secondary school some girls did have relationships with men — they never said whether they slept with them, but they were definitely looked down on; they were called tarts. I was called a lesbian all the time. 'Bender' was the word in use at the time — it was because I got into metal work. I had lots of rows and stuff, and eventually the headmistress said I could do it. I started blacksmithing, and used to change into trousers. It was also at about this time that I started thinking I was a bloke. My Mum was always on at me to wear a skirt. When I got to a certain age when I wouldn't, I'd only wear trousers, my mum used to get really upset and cry and things. My Dad used to have talks with me and say, "Why don't you wear a skirt like all the other girls around here?" One night I got this phone call, and these blokes said, "Did your Mum ever tell you that you looked like a bloke?' That phone call really upset me, I felt like there were enemies all around. It became more difficult to turn up at school. School was one big nightmare.

I never had a relationship with a man. I came close to, but decided that I'd rather be in bed with a woman. I just can't remember ever having feelings for blokes. The reason I wanted to be one was because they seemed to have a good time. Women just seemed to accept whatever was coming to them. Blokes just seemed the only interesting ones around. It was only recently that I discovered why they could be more interesting — they had more freedom. My brothers had more freedom than I did. They still do. And I was surrounded by women who just accepted that, because of the community.

I remember at school, having all these 'best friends' and then they'd go off with a bloke. I used to go home crying. My Mum would say, "What's wrong?", and I'd say "My best friend has gone off with a bloke". She'd say, "Well that's what happens — it'll happen to you." I thought, "I don't want to accept this!" I felt this way all through school. I looked up homosexual in the library. I wanted to know why I felt this way. It was only in the most diabolical books on 'Youth Delinquency'. In these books they said stuff like: with women it's butch and femme. Saying things like — "It is easier to understand the women who desire to be butch, because they want to be men, the ones that are more difficult to understand are the femme women. We find this a phenomenon which is difficult to understand . . . It may be to do with hormones.' So I developed this theory that it was my hormones.

I then got hold of my first lesbian book — I heard my Mum talking about it — it was Radcliffe Hall's 'The Well of Loneliness'. Basically it is just one big advertisement not to be a dyke. I mean, it was really heavy. I really like that book now. It's a classic, and I see it as an historical book about one woman's really brave struggle. But then I thought, "Oh, is this what it has come to?'. I thought that I could get into it. I started wearing a suit — not completely modern, I was getting nattier now, I used to grease my hair back sometimes.

I left school and decided 'I've got to get to London, I know that there are other gay people in London.' I thought I've just got to get out of here. I'd had a relationship with a woman in London when I was younger. We both got into drugs together. She lived in Lambeth. We were both into heroin and stuff. Then I had to make a decision — either to stay with her and take lots of drugs, or try to get myself off the drugs. I decided to straighten out and get into my art, and go to college (in London) — my passport to freedom.

I got involved in WAGS, it was very much the straight dyke scene — butch and femme. I thought, "Which one am I going to be?" I thought "I'm not into being femme, so I'll be butch." I'd played roles before, and had an S/M relationship with a woman before, and I'm still into that, although I've been through the whole head trip the feminists put onto S/M dykes. But I think that it's really important for women to go through whatever painful process and decide where they want to further their sexuality. I don't think I'd oppress any woman. I wouldn't force someone to go to bed with me and to whip her — which isn't my idea of S/M anyway. I'm talking about things that I really care about, and I'm talking about it because I want people to know about my experience. I want people to know where S/M dykes come from, and that it may even be similar to where they come from. I've worked out a lot of personal freedom through S/M, worked out a lot of things about religion and things; and found it really progressive.

We had really crummy places to meet. I was getting depressed about it. I began to think I was a criminal and an outlaw cos look at the places we had to go. We had nowhere that was decent — always red light districts, or crummy cellar bars, or tucked away at the top. There were mainly older women there — they were really into me 'cos I was like a symbol of the future.

There was a lot I envied about the male gay scene. The dykes always seemed to dress down. I wanted a bit of glamour, 'cos the rest of my life was so drab. I went to a disco last week — a mixed night, the place was full of straights, really oppressive heterosexuals taking over the scene and I thought — typical — they've got every fashionable trendy bar to go to and they come here 'cos it's a bit, I've heard the word is *demi-monde*, underground.

I left college half way through. I didn't have that sort of education build-up. I couldn't get into half the ways they thought about things. I was a sort of freak who somehow managed to get into college. I was quite interesting to them. Once I saw how I fitted in, I then saw how I didn't fit in anymore.

College was the passport out of home. I couldn't have stayed at home for much longer. But at that time I really wanted to talk about it. I was used to talking about quite a lot of things, and it was awful that I couldn't talk to her about it. I feel that Mum wouldn't want me in the house. I was too confused and untogether with the drugs to set up a place on my own. I couldn't risk telling them. I remember telling my Mum when I was 12 that I fancied women. And she went, "What? What do you mean? When you see a woman walking down the street do you look at her and think of her sexually?" And it just wasn't what I meant at all. What I was talking about was more subtle, more meaningful than that, even at 12. As soon as she put it in those terms I felt sick. She was describing me as an animal. I never spoke to her about it until last year. I was going out on my own and she called me a hussy, said I was going out to pick up men, have sex with them. I said "There's not a lot of blokes at this place." She said, "I know, it's one of those lesbian set-ups, isn't it? I think it's disgusting. I don't like to think of you getting involved in all that scene, that lesbian scene. You know it's wrong, morally wrong." But then she thinks being unemployed is morally wrong.

I live a political life. I could never slip back into straight life. There's not a place for me there. Most things about that society are completely sick. I suppose I would define myself as feminist, but there are a lot of things feminists would disagree with me about. But that's because they've come from a totally different place. Half of them don't even know the struggle of being a dyke at school, to go to those diabolical places, without the back-up of books and things.

I don't think I can tell everyone that I was seriously going to have a sex change when I came to London. It's something I still feel really embarrassed about saying, it really was a foolish thing. What a way to think! But how else could I see it, without information? As a woman you look at blokes and they've got all the power, and especially if you don't see that there is that much wrong with society, you see yourself as the sick one. In a way it's easier to see yourself like that,'cos once you see that society is sick, and you're still in it and maybe can't do much to change it, then it can be really depressing. I think a lot of women have a sex change to make more sense of what is going on around them. I don't want a bloke's body anymore. But some women, like me, who have grown up in a very strict religious family, where women's bodies are very much hated. I still find it hard to look at my breasts. I'm only just beginning to get less frozen about certain parts of the body which are obviously female.

SANDY, 20.

From very young I always felt I was different, but I didn't know why. I always preferred to play with boys' toys rather than with girls' from as young as I can remember. My parents were really worried about this. I remember them sitting down and having a talk with me one evening, I was about 9 or 10. I carried on the same way until I reached secondary school. Still preferring to wear jeans rather than a frilly dress.

Then I started my second job. I was 18. And fell in love with a woman there. I was very interested in her, I wanted to get to know her. She was 7 years older than me and at that time, as far as I knew, straight. I didn't know how to go about getting to know her. She was in a position of power and I was a pleb. I worked there for about a year and my feelings for her grew and grew 'till it became an obsession in the end. I hated the job, and the guy I worked for was a real pig, but I stayed there just because she was there. I found out that she was leaving and going to Africa with a friend of hers to work. I couldn't cope with it so I found myself another job and left — two weeks after hearing.

She was due to leave a month and a half after I left, and on my last day when it came to say goodbye, I couldn't hold it back — I just cried and cried. She gave me a card with her home number on. So I rang her that weekend and she took my address and said that she'd send a surprise for me. Two days later I received a ticket for a gig in London. I rang her again before the concert and thanked her. She suggested that I stay at her place that night because it would be a hassle to get back to Bexley Heath from central London.

So I went along to this gig. I met up with her and her friend, 'S'. We went back to their place after the gig, and we had a chat and it was great, it was really good. She was so different from the person she was at work. I slept on the floor. She slept in the double bed with her friend. All this time I.

41

was wondering whether they were 'just good friends'. The following morning she explained that it was her friend who was going to work in Africa and she'd like a holiday, so she was going along for six months. I saw her again the day before her friend, 'S', left for Africa. There was another month before she left. During that time I saw her about twice a week. One evening after about 20 bottles of wine, she crashed out on the bed and I was just sitting next to her staring straight ahead of me. She asked me what was on my mind and I just said, "I can't tell you." She said, "I hope you can tell me one day'. Then she said, "Give me a cuddle." So I did. And it just went from there. She then said it was the first time that she had been with a woman. Then she asked me a question which really disturbed me. She said, "You've never got on with your mother, have you?". I said, "What are you trying to dig up?" She replied, "There's nothing to dig up, is there?" Then she just gave me a kiss goodnight and went to sleep. I slept with her again, once more, the following week. It just happened and we didn't talk about it the next morning. It was as though it hadn't happened. I left her that day in tears because I was going to see her just once more before she flew out. There were all these things I wanted to say, I just didn't know how.

I saw her the day before she flew off. We were both really happy and positive about everything. She said she'd write to me as soon as she could. I received a letter every week, and sent one every week. She told me to start evening classes to learn German, because she was German. After she returned from Africa she was going back to Germany and wanted me to join her. So I started German classes. And thought about her every day. I phoned her once when she was in Africa. Twenty-five minutes we talked. It was just really good to hear her voice. She had planned the next ten years of my life.

I got a phone call one day from a guy who said that he was a good friend of hers, and that he had something to tell me. So he travelled from North London to Bexley Heath, and I met up with him. He explained that her friend, 'S'. and her had been driving through the bush, and a tyre had burst. She hadn't been wearing a seat belt, The car went out of control and she was killed instantly. 'S', who was driving, had been wearing a seat belt and only got a few bruises.

I was numb. I just got out of the car and walked. I don't know where I walked. I ended up in a park. I hadn't cried 'till I got there, then I cried 'till I thought I was going to be sick. After that I just went home and climbed into bed and stayed there for about three days. My parents and friends couldn't understand why I was so upset, 'cos they hadn't known her, or known of our friendship.

I went to the funeral in Munich, which was arranged by 'S', she arranged my flight too. I spent a week in Munich with her parents. I spoke to 'S'. I said we were very close, I didn't tell her 'cos I thought I'd be opening up a side of 'B' that her friend hadn't known. From then on I spent a lot of time with 'S'. I went back to work. I cut off from all my friends. I started drinking and smoking too much dope. I felt as though I had nothing left, absolutely nothing.

After a few months, I had to talk to someone about it, knowing that I was a lesbian, I wanted to speak to other lesbians. So I rang a number in City Limits and went to a group. I've been going there for the past two months. I've got so much support from them, they've really helped me through it.

I'm coping, going to college in September, as 'B' wanted me to, and thankful to her for helping me to discover the real me.

KIM, 17.

They say, 'What is wrong with her? Haven't we given her all that a girl could want?' But it has come to the point, that what I now need in life, they will never understand, never try to come to terms with or accept. They want me to bow down to convention, be something I am not. If I do not conform to this, I am a failure in their eyes. I know now that I shall never fulfil their expectations, that they will disown me... I feel so suffocated, unable to avoid the hurt, to express my feelings freely. Will I have to play the game, keep up the pretence for the rest of my life? Must I always feel an outsider, struggling alone with my inner emotional torture, plagued and frustrated by those around me? Am I fated to carry my secret loneliness with me forever, a victim of a social order, which has caused me to lose all sense of being an individual person? When I wake up, I feel life is unbearable, that I have been given a cross to bear which I strive to carry on my shoulders all day. Am I a fool to imagine that there might be some place in the world where I can be down to earth about myself with the knowledge that there are people around me who understand, who perhaps even admire and love me. I honestly find I can no longer be anything but myself, feeling like a butterfly, which has to escape the isolation of its cocoon.

LIZ, 18.

From the word go I liked other little girls (and boys). Of course, this was OK, it was only a phase I would soon grow out of. I didn't. Until people pointed it out to me, I never realised I was a pervert. Then, in a classic case of over compensation, I became a raving (heterosexual) nymphomaniac. Soon, I was convinced I was "in love", and was spending about 12 hours a day in bed, going through Masters and Johnson. Everything was hunkydory. But it wasn't.

Speaking of lust, my stepfather was attracted to me and tried to seduce me, with money, clothes. He forced me to eat in expensive restaurants with him, to nightclub, to ride in his big black cadillac, a gangster's Moll. He was very dominant, macho, violent. A crop or a fist, it was all the same to him. I had to submit as he mentally raped me, sexually assaulted me. I hated him. I hated myself. I wanted him dead.

Isolated, depressed, and terrified of rejection by everyone from my mother to the milkman, I became obsessed with my problems, paranoid, haunted by guilt. My lesbianism was a lifeline to sanity — what was happening didn't hurt so much, because it was outside of my own emotional experience. I forced it to be. But if you give me the "bad experience" trip, I swear I'll scream. I already was a lesbian, it just speeded things up a lot. OK, so a lesbian identity was mental armour, but it was thickened rather than forged. These memories are very painful.

Anyway, after being fucked up for months, I pulled myself together enough to ring Lesbian Line. The relief of not being the only one was overwhelming. Initially, my clandestine lesbian contacts were just targets to direct my anger and guilt at, and people to rudely ask exactly what it was THEY did in bed. Then one day I realised that THEY were human, too.

University offered an escape from home — of sorts.. At a predominantly male college (real women don't do sciences) I met immature, macho, public school brats out to prove something. We didn't have a lot in common. The girls were worse. Homophobia was rampant. I felt like a freak. I hated it. I dropped out.

Hall was as bad. Fed up of living a lie, I came out to a few women (it was all-female). One girl came along to a women's bar and then freaked out on me. Word spread. QUICKLY. I was an object of horror and fascination. I got very pissed off. I decided to give them something to talk about, and began to stalk around in leather, studs, shades. Menacingly. Underneath, I felt very vulnerable.

I drifted. To the "Scene", eventually, which is where I am now. With one or two reservations, I'm probably the happiest I've ever been. I've met some great women.

'Dear Debbie. . .'

I started to write
It's been a cold and lonely night
I put the pen down.
My mind's in turmoil
My face a permanent frown.

I've known you for so long
3 years now — or maybe I'm wrong
But it seems like just the other day
You 'came out' and told me you were gay.

This strengthened the bond between us,
I loved and understood you more.
My mother asked if I was.
I told her I wasn't sure.

I met a girl with a delicate nature
She turned that frown into a smile.
I'm hoping I'll never hurt her
And it will last a while.

But does this mean I'm gay?
Do I know the meaning of the word?
Maybe it's too early to say
Is it an echo I've heard.

Then there was Mike
People try not to stare
His painted face so feminine
Framed with a black cascade of hair

I found the reason.
Classification if you like.
I'm bi-sexual.
Not straight or a dyke.

EMMA, 17

VICKY, 18.

I came out four months ago — in March 1984, and in a space of two weeks of going to my first all womens bar, I had told my parents and my best friends. I felt with my brother also being gay, I had a pillar to lean against when things got rough at home.

I was fortunate in the respect that my brother had a lodger who was a lesbian, and she took me to my first bar. My brother had realised that I was a lesbian when I was in my early teenage years and after going to his house one night they discussed it and Josette said that she would ask me to the Drill Hall, (A women only bar). I was very apprehensive at first, but soon realised that everyone was friendly and very helpful in discussing my sexuality.

Dad was away on business up North so I rang my brother and told him I had come out to Mum and he came home from the office. My Mum's reaction to him was that he had indoctrinated me into it. My brother managed to calm my Mum down and raised a smile when he said, 'Don't worry, you've got a matching set now.' Dad had heard that something was wrong at home via the office and started to drive home immediately. When he got home my Mum went into another state of hysteria. Unfortunately Dad and Mum brought each other down instead of trying to support each other.

I stayed at my brother's that night leaving my sister to cope with Mum and Dad. When we left the house my Dad had just started to drink. For the next few weeks my Mum wouldn't sit in the same room as me and I felt rejected. However, life got better but to every high point in the week there would be two low points. I feel now that it would be better for me to move out because my Mum said that she can't cope with me staying out the night and she felt I was just using the house as a hotel.

Final Comment

I can't write this final comment in the third person, this is not a textbook or research paper. There is a lot of pain and hurt in these pages. Putting these quotes and stories together hasn't been from a removed position. I have come to know a number of these young women and have developed a great respect for them, and very often a fondness too. I've felt hurt, angry and guilty about some of the things these young lesbians have said. Hurt for the pain many have gone through (often alone and unsupported), anger about the way that society has treated young women who love (just because they love other women), guilt because I am part of that society which isn't doing enough for these young women.

The young lesbians have shown themselves to be aware and worthy of admiration. They have had to think through the question of their sexuality, often against prevailing attitudes and ignorance. They have a mature attitude to life, and have questioned the values and assumptions of society with clarity and understanding. They have not merely criticised society, but have made constructive suggestions for changing it, not only to make things better for themselves, but for everyone.

I think what impressed me (and affected me) most was the way that these young women coped with what often seemed intolerable situations. They survived through crises few older people would without the support of society. Rejected by parents, or coping with being institutionalised. Dealing with alienation, harassment, break-ups, and, not least, death — without having a shoulder to cry on, without people to talk to, to share the hurt, without the support of family, the understanding of teachers. AND STILL EMERGING POSITIVE ABOUT THEIR SEXUALITY.

Homosexuality is not a problem, other people's reaction to it is. These young women have suffered because of society's prejudice and survived as strong individuals. I think young lesbians are brill.

CONTACT LIST

London Lesbian Line: 01 251 6911: 2-10pm Monday and Friday, 7-10pm Tuesday, Wednesday and Thursday.

Other Lesbian Lines:

Bangor	0248 351263	Tuesdays 8-10pm
Birmingham	021 6226580	Mondays and Wednesdays 7-10pm
Bradford	0274 305525	Thursdays 7-9pm
Bradford	0274 723802	Wednesdays 7-10pm
Belfast	0232 222023	Thursdays 7.30-9.30pm
Brighton	0273 603298	Tuesdays 8-10pm, Fridays 2-5pm then 8-10pm
Bristol	0272 425927	Wednesday 8-10pm
Cambridge	0223 246113	Friday 6-10pm
Cardiff	0222 374051	Thursdays 8-10pm
Colchester	0206 870051	Wednesdays 8-10pm
Coventry	0203 77105	Wednesdays 7-10pm
Dublin	0001 710608	Thursday 8-10pm
Edinburgh	031 5564049	Thursdays 7.30-10pm
Glasgow	041 2484596	Monday 7-10pm
Leeds	0532 453488	Tuesdays 7.30-9.30pm
Leicester	0533 826299	Nightly 7.30-10.30pm
Liverpool	051 7080234	Tuesdays and Thursdays 7-10.30pm
Manchester	061 2366205	Monday to Thursday 7-10pm
Merseyside	074 434920	Monday and Thursday 8.30-11pm
Newcastle	0632 612277	Thursday & Friday 7-10pm
Oxford	0865 24233	Wednesday 7-10pm
Norwich	0603 28055	Tuesdays 8-10pm
Peterborough	0733 238005	Nightly 'till 10pm
Sheffield	0742 581238	Thursdays 7-10pm
Swansea	0792 467365	Friday 7-9pm

Also

Young Lesbian Group: 01 263 5932: North London. 7.30-10.30pm Monday. Youth club and phone line for young lesbians (16-21 years old).

London Gay Teenage Group: 01 272 5741: 3-7pm Sunday, 7-10pm Wednesday. Youth club and phone line in North London for 16-21 year olds.

South London Young Gay Peoples Group: 01 697 7435. 7-10pm Mondays. Youth club and phone line in the Lewisham area.

South London Young Lesbian Group: 01 697 7435. Tuesdays. As above.

Gay Youth Movement: c/o BM GYM, London WC1N 3XX. (For those under 26 years old). Can put you in touch with local gay youth groups.

London Friend (Women's Line) 01 345 1846. 7.30-1opm Thursdays.

Gay Switchboard: 01 837 7324, 24 hours a day every day.

Parents Enquiry: 01 698 1815, helps families through the traumas of coming out. Any reasonable time.

BOOK LIST

NOVELS:
Happy endings are all alike by Sandra Scopperttone
Hey Dollface by Deborah Hautzig
Patience and Sarah by Isabel Miller
Rubyfruit Jungle by Rita Mae Brown
Fox Running by K nudson
Fox Running by K nudson
The Colour Purple by Alice Walker

INFORMATION:
"Something to tell you . . ." by Lorraine Trenchard and Hugh Warren
The Lesbian Primer by Liz Diamond
Sappho Was A Right-On-Woman by Sidney Abbot and Barbara Love
Young, Gay and Proud Alyson Publications
Girls are Powerful: Young Women's writing from Spare Rib edited by Susan Hemmings
Nice Jewish girls: A Lesbian Anthology edited by Evelyn Torton Beck

BOOKSHOPS
Sisterwrite, 190 Upper Street, London N.1 Tel : 01 226 9782
Silver Moon, 68 Charing Cross Road, London WC2. Tel 01-836 7906
Gay's the Word, 66 Marchmont Street, London WC1. Tel 01-278 7654